The *Motivated* Job Search Workbook

Job Search Exercises for *The Motivated Job Search* and *Over 50 and Motivated!* Job Search Books

Brian E. Howard, JD, CCMC, CJSS, CPRW
Certified Career Management Coach
Certified Job Search Strategist
Certified Professional Resume Writer

Virginia

The external links are being provided as a convenience and for informational purposes only; they do not constitute an endorsement or an approval by BQB Publishing, WriteLife Publishing or the author of any of the products, services or opinions of the corporation or organization or individual. BQB Publishing, WriteLife Publishing, and the author bear no responsibility for the accuracy, legality, or content of the external site or for that of subsequent links. Contact the external site for answers to questions regarding its content.

The information and recommendations in this book are presented in good faith and for informational purposes only. Every effort has been made to ensure the materials presented are accurate and current. All information is supplied on the condition that the reader or any other person receiving this information will perform their own due diligence and make their own determination as to its suitability for any purpose prior to the use of this information. The purpose of this material is to educate. The author, Brian E. Howard, and/or any affiliated companies, shall have neither liability nor responsibility to any person or entity with respect to loss or damage caused, or alleged to have been caused, directly or indirectly, by the information contained in this book.

Published in the United States by WriteLife Publishing
(An imprint of Boutique of Quality Books Publishing Company)
www.writelife.com

Printed in the United States of America

978-1-60808-179-0 (p)
978-1-60808-180-6 (e)

Library of Congress Control Number: 2016963664
Book design by Robin Krauss, www.bookformatters.com
Cover design by Ellis Dixon, ellisdixon.com
Editor: Paige Duke

LinkedIn, the LinkedIn logo, the IN logo and InMail are registered trademarks of LinkedIn Corporation and its affiliates in the Unisted States and/or other countries.

OTHER BOOKS BY BRIAN E. HOWARD

The Motivated Job Search

The Motivated Networker

Over 50 and Motivated!

Motivated Resumes and LinkedIn Profiles

MESSAGE FROM THE AUTHOR

The actual number of hours you will spend conducting a job search compared to the actual number of hours you spend involved in duties and responsibilities of your career is a sliver of time. This is especially true when you consider that many people are choosing to work longer and careers are now lasting forty to fifty years! In very broad (unscientific) terms, the amount of time you spend committed to a job search could be one to six months of actual time in a forty- to fifty-year career. When you consider the ramifications of a job search against career enjoyment and financial earning power, the importance of a well-planned and well-executed job search becomes apparent.

I wrote this workbook to work in conjunction with *The Motivated Job Search* and *Over 50 and Motivated!* books. The writing exercises are designed to make you think about your career and your job search, and to serve as a platform to create and organize information. When you use this workbook in conjunction with either of the job search books, you can rest assured that you have the information to plan and execute a Self-Motivated Job Search in the most effective and efficient way possible.

To your success!
Brian E. Howard

Table of Contents

Your Job Search Arsenal: Tools and Tactics

The following is a reasonably comprehensive, though not necessarily exhaustive, list of considerations, tools, and tactics for a Self-Motivated Job Search. The checklist is designed as a visual reminder of the tools and tactics at your disposal during your job search. Use it as a checklist as you prepare for your search as well as action items to guide you through your search. Consult the job search books (*The Motivated Job Search* and *Over 50 and Motivated!*) for in-depth information.

It's recommended that you review this list periodically as a reminder of what you should be doing or can be doing to advance your job search.

Item	Comments	Check-off √
Covenant-not-to-compete Non-solicitation agreement	Adjust your job search if you have either of these	
Cleanse all social media sites	Delete all inappropriate pictures and comments	
Emotions—positive attitude	Stay away from negative thoughts and feelings. Positive attitude. Gratitude list.	
Resume (See checklist)	It is imperative to have an impactful resume	
LinkedIn profile (See checklist)	Like a resume, an impactful LinkedIn profile is imperative to your job search	

Business Cards
   Traditional
   Networking
   Resume
   Infographic
	Select the one(s) you will use in your search	

Exit Statement	Script for social events and one for interviews	
Target Opportunity Profile	Know what job(s) you're looking for	
Keywords	Know the keywords that apply to you	
Job Alerts	Indeed, SimplyHired, LinkedIn, Job boards, Twitter, others	

Item	Comments	Check-off √
Master Job Description	Doing this helps you think like the hiring executive	
Accomplishments	Know what accomplishments differentiate you	
Transferable Skills and Professional Qualities	Know those skills and qualities that make you truly unique and are often sought after by employers.	
Success Stories	Pre-write three. Helps in interviews and answering behavior-based questions.	
Branding	Those words and statements that announce to the market who you are and what you offer.	
Elevator speech	Who you are, what you do, accomplishments, start a conversation, scripted and practiced.	
Cover letter	Write a template then modify. Similar to a marketing email.	
List target employers	Create a list. Add new employers when they are discovered.	
Short-list of networking contacts	Your Cabinet, plus others	

Networking
    Local events
    National conference
    Online
    Research interviews, etc.
	A high percentage of all jobs are found through some form of networking.	

Icebreaker questions	Prepared in advance of networking events. Having them reduces anxiety for networking events.	
Recruiters	Identified and contacted	

Proactively marketing your professional credentials by phone
    Script marketing call
    Voicemail script
    Responses to objections
    Script for handling the gatekeeper
	This approach drives straight into the heart of the hidden job market. It is the most direct method for getting interviews.	

Proactively marketing your professional credentials by Email (InMail)
    Write email message
    Script follow-up call
	Another effective approach that works to discover jobs in the hidden job market. Always follow up with a phone call.	

Drip marketing	Used to stay in touch with a hiring executive with new information	

Item	Comments	Check-off √
Last ditch effort email	Last email contact to a hiring executive that is not responding	

Interviewing
  Scripted answers to common questions
  Scripted answers for anticipated questions
  Research
	A lot of information about interviewing. Prepare for common or anticipated questions. Do research before every interview.	

References	Wisely chosen and listed. Unsolicited third-party affirmation technique	
Brag Book	Differentiation tactic	
Career Summary Sheet	Differentiation tactic	
Testimonial Sheet	Differentiation tactic	
Action Plan	Differentiation tactic	
Personal website	Differentiation tactic	
Blog	Differentiation tactic	
Infographic resume	Differentiation tactic	
Direct U.S. Mail contact to hiring executives	Traditional approach. Can be useful for hard-to-reach hiring executives or as a last ditch effort.	
Career Fairs	Useful for some levels of positions	
Emotion—rejection	Disappointments will happen. Continue to move forward. Don't get stuck!	
Career Transition Coach	For in-depth job search advice, accountability, insight	
Effort	Stay busy! 30 hours/week if unemployed, 6 to 8 hours/week if employed	
Avoid busywork	Focus on those tasks that truly advance your search. Your heart will know the difference.	
Volunteering, consulting	If unemployed, volunteer or do paid consulting projects. Some employers view volunteering equal to work experience.	
Relying solely on posted job openings	Will significantly lengthen your job search and tear down your self-confidence	**X – No!**

FOR TENURED JOB SEEKERS

What You're Up Against

There are several biases that tenured job seekers face. These include: the perception of a bad attitude, inflexible, tired, "on cruise control" to retirement, weak technology skills, entitlement mentality, poor cultural fit (with younger employees), being able to report to a younger boss, poor communication skills, out-of-date appearance, and high compensation and benefit requirements.

These biased perceptions can be an obstacle to your job search, and they are unfair. However, being honest with yourself and acknowledging your potential weaknesses is the first step to combating these biases in your search. You can take steps to improve.

 Take some time and honestly assess yourself against these common biases. Do any of these actually apply to you? Write them down.

Now, think of action items, real steps you can take to improve in these areas. Some may be easier to resolve than others. For example, for appearance it could be as simple as buying new clothes. But an entitlement mentality . . . well, that could take more concentrated effort because it requires a change in attitude.

 List what you can commit to doing to counterbalance any known biases. Writing down these action items will help you put them in motion.

Advantages of Your Age (Tenure)

For tenured job seekers, there are far more advantages to your age and tenure than there are age biases. These include: judgment, reliability, work ethic, critical thinking, ability to read people, network, less job supervision, market knowledge, commitment to quality, professionalism, confidence, wisdom, stability, experience, accomplishments, and loyalty.

There are likely other advantages that might be unique to you. Write them down!

 List the advantages of your tenure that apply to you. Some will likely come from the list above, but include any that you've thought of as well.

Now, from the list you made, think of an on-the-job example of when you used those professional traits or skills. This step is important. To be effective, you must be able to relay a story or short example that exemplifies that professional characteristic. It is embarrassing if a hiring executive asks you for a real-life example of a professional trait and you stumble though a contrived answer. The hiring executive will see right through that.

 Write down short stories and examples of your professional traits in action. (Refer also to the Success Stories topic in *The Motivated Job Search* and *Over 50 and Motivated!* and this workbook.)

Emotions

If you lost your job, especially if it happened unexpectedly, it is an emotional event. Attached to the job loss comes loss of identity, self-esteem, friendships with those at work, possible embarrassment, feelings of no longer being productive, loss of a sense of purpose, loss of a sense of control, emptiness, not to mention the change in your daily routine. It's okay to be angry, and it is certainly okay to cry—as often as you need to. To have a proper attitude for your job search, you must have your emotions in check. If you do not, it will be reflected in subtle ways, in your writings, in your interviews, in social interactions, among others.

If you feel as if you may be harboring negative emotions, one helpful technique is to write about your feelings. Forget about the grammar and spelling. Start writing and don't hold back! Any negative feelings that come into your mind go down in writing.

 Start writing about any negative feelings you may have.

Gratitude List

Another effective technique that can diffuse negative emotions of a job loss is a gratitude list. A gratitude list is all the things (personal, professional, spiritual, and so on) that you are grateful for. Include all things in your life. Good starting points can be family, experiences, vacations, faith, and so many others. Start writing everything down, regardless of how small. Add to the list over time. Re-read the list when you are feeling blue or defeated about your job search.

 Writing a gratitude list often puts things in perspective and can lift your spirits. It can often stop the "parade of terribles" in your mind. Start listing what you are grateful for.

Future Opportunities and Blessings to Come

So far, as we have been dealing with the emotions of a job loss, we have released the negative emotions and vented our feelings by writing it all down. To counter-balance all those negative emotions, we started a gratitude list of all of the things in life we are grateful for. Hopefully the gratitude list reminds you of all the good things you have in life.

Now to complete the process, start thinking about the opportunities and blessings that lie before you. This list (writing exercise) is future looking. Start thinking about the good things that could come from or will come as a result of your job change. Start dreaming and imagining a better or more suitable job. This includes all positive things you can think of as well as the elimination of some of the bad things from your previous jobs (e.g., "I don't have to put up with long-winded John anymore!") Open your mind to the possibilities.

 Start listing and writing about the blessings and opportunities to come. Start writing and dreaming about what your future could be.

THE ADVANTAGES OF A
SELF-MOTIVATED JOB SEARCH

The Motivated Job Search and *Over 50 and Motivated!* list and discuss several advantages of a Self-Motivated Job Search.

 As you read through the list of advantages, which ones were more impactful or influential regarding your own job search and why?

 Are there other advantages you can think of that would apply to your personal job search? If so, write them down.

The point of this exercise is this: Having an intellectual understanding and appreciation for an action-driven, self-motivated job search strategy can significantly shorten your job search and get you back to work and receiving a routine paycheck. However, relying on posted online openings or otherwise taking a passive lackadaisical job search strategy will dramatically lengthen your job search by potentially months or longer. Only you can make the decision of which approach you will take and the action or inaction of your chosen strategy.

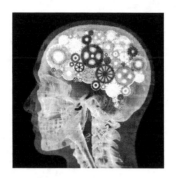

THE PSYCHOLOGY OF PERSUASION

The psychology of persuasion is discussed in detail in *The Motivated Job Search* and *Over 50 and Motivated!* There is not too much to be done on this topic from a preparation and writing exercises standpoint. However, since this deals with psychology, the concepts here are not so much in the tangible realm but reach into the subliminal.

Raising your awareness of the principles of persuasion during your job search is a good use of your time.

The Scarcity Principle. If a hiring executive views you as unique or special, you are seen as more valuable. This is the Scarcity principle, and it is created by differentiating yourself from others.

Much of *The Motivated Job Search* and *Over 50 and Motivated!* is centered around differentiation. This not only includes how you present yourself as a professional job seeker but also the job search tactics you will employ.

 To kick-start your thinking, list five things that differentiate you from other job seekers. Trust that as you work your way through *The Motivated Job Search* and *Over 50 and Motivated!*, you will think of more.

1.

2.

3.

4.

5.

The Authority Principle. Most people respond to authority. This can come in various forms such as title, education, experience, and so on. *The Motivated Job Search* and *Over 50 and Motivated!* list interviewing attire as possibly triggering an authority (respect) response during an interview. Now, humbly think about yourself.

 What elements of your professional life could elevate you in the eyes of an employer and trigger the persuasion principle of authority (respect)?

The Liking (Personal Chemistry) Principle. Sixty percent of most hires are based on personal chemistry. Hiring executives hire people they have a personal liking for.

Personal chemistry can be created between strangers by finding common ground. People who look for common interests and topics tend to make friends more quickly and easily. *The Motivated Job Search* and *Over 50 and Motivated!* list six ways to establish commonality with a hiring executive.

 Review the list, but think of others ways you might be able to establish rapport.

The Social Proof Principle. What others say about you is more persuasive than what you say about yourself. This is social proof.

 Think about where in your job search you could use a recommendation or affirmation to advance your job search. You could be surprised where and how often it could be used.

Consistency and Commitment. People want a reputation of sticking to their word. The Persuasion Principle of Consistency and Commitment is in play when a hiring executive makes a commitment to a course of action.

 Think and write down a couple of situations where you could use this persuasion principle in your job search.

Reciprocation (Reciprocity). There is a strong motivation to return favors and not feel indebted to others. We want to repay others for their kindness and for what they do for us. This is the Reciprocation Principle.

The Motivated Job Search and *Over 50 and Motivated!* list a couple of examples where you (as the job seeker) can offer something for free during a job search. During your search, be aware of things you can do or provide, or ways you can assist the hiring executive. Do so without expecting anything in return (but knowing that the reciprocation principle is present. Besides, doing this is also good networking and creates good karma.).

Think and write down some ideas for reciprocity. You may need to be creative.

As previously mentioned, the purpose of this section is to raise your awareness of the Persuasion Principles. In this way you will be using psychology as another tactic in your job search.

YOUR CAREER . . . YOUR RESPONSIBILITY

This topic in *The Motivated Job Search* and *Over 50 and Motivated!* lists six perspectives about your career. They are:

1. I am solely responsible for my career success.

2. It is my responsibility to enhance my value proposition.

3. I must deliver an ROI (Return on Investment).

4. I am responsible for my work-life balance.

5. It is my responsibility to stay informed about the financial health and well-being of my employer and the industry in which I work.

6. Change is inevitable in my career. How I respond to change is completely within my control.

 As you read and pondered these career perspectives, which were particularly impactful or informative to you? Why?

Which of these perspectives caused you to think about your career going forward? How?

The purpose of this exercise is to raise your awareness about the ownership responsibility you have to your career and your job search. Being aware and proactive with your career's status (health) will help you flourish and help prevent negative career events and surprises.

YOUR EXIT STATEMENT

Having a rehearsed Exit Statement is important. It can save you from awkward moments when asked about your employment status. The key points to remember about your Exit Statement are:

1. **Keep it aligned.** Make sure your statement reflects what happened and what your former employer may say.

2. **Keep it positive.** Do not make any negative statements about your former company, boss, and colleagues.

3. **Keep it factual.** Do not unload emotions into your explanation.

4. **Keep it short.** Do not get into an extended explanation. Make your statement and be done.

Here are some good explanations for networking and social settings:

- "The company went through a reorganization."

- "The company was purchased."

- "The company had to make budget cuts, and there were departmental layoffs. I was a casualty."

- "Based on company direction, we mutually agreed to part ways."

Write down your networking and social setting Exit Statement.

During interviews, especially with key hiring executives, a one- or two-sentence Exit Statement simply will not suffice. You need to say more. Below is an example of a more thorough Exit Statement for those circumstances:

I was hired four years ago to build the sales structure and process to put Up-and-Comer, Inc. on a solid growth trajectory. I was responsible for driving the strategies that generated a 40+% software revenue and a robust client base increase from 92 to over 650 clients including an increase from 2 to 9 Fortune 50 clients. In 20XX, we achieved 100% client revenue retention.

Our current CEO is the founder of the company. He is a brilliant man with a passionate vision for Up-and-Comer's position in the market and society. It has been a delight and a privilege to be his partner in achieving the company's status as a proven, transformative solution for employers.

I am still invested in Up-and-Comer's success, however, over the course of the last [a time frame] the CEO and I reached a conclusion that we had different visions regarding the direction of the company. Together we agreed that it was time I move on. So the CEO and I amicably agreed to a severance arrangement from the company.

 Using this example as a conceptual guide to your thinking, write your detailed Exit Statement. Keep your statement around 175–200 words. You should be able to deliver it in 60 to 90 seconds.

PROFILING YOUR NEXT
CAREER OPPORTUNITY

One of the more important things to do as you begin your job search is knowing what you're looking for. For some, this is a reasonably easy task. For others, it can be bewildering.

For those job seekers wanting to explore an entirely different career direction but are unsure of what they want, there is an insightful exercise that can help identify possible career paths. It's called a Passions Inventory. It may not give you all of the answers you seek, however it will give structure to your thinking and possibly get you pointed in the right direction.

To start the exercise, compensation and prerequisite education are not to be limiting factors. This is "free-form" exploration. Remove practicality from the equation, at least for the moment (practicality plays a part later).

 Starting your Passions Inventory. List what you enjoy doing—personally or professionally. List what captures and holds your attention. What do you think about, read, listen to, watch? This could include things you enjoy from past employment. Hobbies can be insightful here. No item is too small.

The next step is to add a little practicality into the mix. Ask yourself what skills and abilities you enjoy using. Your skills list can be as long as the interests list you just wrote. It could include such things as writing, sales ability, working with your hands, and many more. Now list the skills you enjoy using.

The final step is to cross-reference and combine. Depending on the length of your two lists, this could be quite an exploration. Where can you use your skill(s) with a passion/interest(s)? Is there a combination of interests and skills that has commercial value? In other words, would someone hire you to do what you enjoy and pay you for it?

Here's where real-life practicality comes into play. You may identify an interest and an accompanying skill but lack the prerequisite education (e.g., a law degree) to pursue the interest. Or there may not be a viable market. For example, you like to weave and you like working with leather—you can make buggy whips! But there's no longer a viable commercial market for that. You get the point.

 Start thinking and cross-referencing your interests and skills lists.

CAREER WISH LIST

This exercise is for job seekers who have a fairly good idea what they might want to do but have some lingering doubts or possible curiosity about other directions. If you think about your career direction, you have five options available to you when you go through a career transition. They are:

1. Same job in the same industry

2. Different job in the same industry

3. Same job in a different industry

4. Different job in a different industry

5. Start your own business

The fourth and fifth options are complete career transitions, and the Passions Inventory could be helpful in those circumstances.

 To help clarify what you may be looking for in your next opportunity, start a Career Wish List. Start this list by listing all of the things you like about your past (and current) jobs. Go through your career and reminisce about all of the things you liked about each position.

Now, list the dislikes for all of your positions. Often it is just as important to know what you don't want as much as what you do want in your next position.

 Once you have listed your dislikes, flip them over and convert them into a "like" if you can. Doing this can occasionally add clarity to what you do want. For example, "I didn't like working for Jim because he was a micromanager." When flipped, it could read like this: "I want to work for someone who doesn't look over my shoulder and lets me do my job." This flipping process can add some depth to your understanding during your job profiling process.

The next step is a list of those things you want in your next position. Through the first three steps, you've created a lot of food for thought. Read over what you've already written and start thinking about the future and your next job. A little daydreaming is encouraged. Write down what you want in your next position.

 The final step is to look at the totality of what you have written (or listed). Mull all of this over and begin to prioritize those things that mean the most to you. As you do this, a mental picture should start to emerge of the profile you are seeking in your next job. Prioritize the more important items you have identified.

Working through the Career Wish List exercise is a mind-opening approach. With a little guidance, you allow your mind to roam free about likes, dislikes (including flipping), and wants. There are more concrete considerations that should also be considered if you have not thought of them already. What follows is a non-exhaustive list of other job profiling consideration. Write down any appropriate thoughts after each consideration.

Skills/Strengths

 What skills (or strengths) do you like using? These are the skills and strengths you enjoy and feel energy and passion when you're using them. What inspires you, fulfills you, and creates that emotional or intellectual "tickle" inside you? When you use these skills and strengths, you often lose track of time. Write down the skills you like using.

Weaknesses/Disinterest

This part of the profiling process is the opposite and has two parts: Identifying those weaknesses you can improve and those weaknesses that are a disinterest to you.

 What skills do you want to improve upon?

On the other hand, areas of weakness that are a disinterest to you are the skills or job functions that are pure drudgery for you.

What skills or job functions are disinteresting for you? (The point here is, it's as important to know what you don't want as it is what you do want.)

Industry

 In what industry do you want to work? Is it the same industry in which you have the most experience? The key issue is the future viability or health of the industry of interest. A few things to consider: Is there growth? Are there new companies entering the market? What are the legislative/legal considerations, both positive and negative? Are there new innovations or products/services to propel those companies ahead of the competition? Write down the industry(ies) in which you want to work.

Function

 What do you want to do in your chosen industry? Your function or role ties into what your unique set of qualifications and overall skill set are. You should feel comfortable—if not downright passionate—about your function or career position. Write down the function or role(s) that you will pursue.

Company

 What does your next employer look like? There are many considerations that may or may not be of any consequence to you, such as:

- Publicly held
- Privately held
- Large
- Small
- Start-up
- Venture-capital backed
- Aggressive growth strategy
- Standing in the industry
- Products—innovative or commoditized

Write down what your next employer may look like.

Location

 Where do you want to work? List the cities, states, or countries where you are willing to live and work. If you are not willing to relocate, simply list the name of your current town or city. If you are willing to move, consider these factors:

- What areas of the country would interest you?
- Are there particular cities you would like to live in?
- Are there family motivations to stay or move?
- What areas of the country would you not relocate to?
- Are international locations a possibility?
- Do you have limitations on commuting time?

Write down location considerations.

Title

How important is a title to you? For some, it has limited importance. For others, it matters more. Here are some things to consider:

- What titles would be acceptable to you?
- Is there a minimum title level you want?
- Is there a titling concept you prefer (e.g., business development versus sales)?
- What about a titling "prefix" (*Senior* Account Manager, *Executive* Vice President)?

Write down your title considerations.

Work Setting

What type of working environment is best for you? List the characteristics of the environment you would like. For example:

- Do you want an office environment?
- Are you comfortable working from a home-based office?
- Are you willing to travel? If so, how much?
- Do you prefer a larger corporate environment?
- Do you like smaller, more entrepreneurial companies?

Write down your work setting considerations.

Compensation and Employee Benefits

 This topic will require serious thought. What would you (realistically) like to be paid? What benefits are important to you? Some issues to consider include:

- What is your minimum salary requirement? How flexible can you be?

- If variable compensation is a component to your overall compensation package, at what level or potential additional earnings?

- Will variable compensation affect your minimum salary requirement? Can you accept a lower salary but be open to more incentive-based pay?

- Employee benefits: Will your family be added to your benefits? Or can you be put on your spouse's insurance plan and thereby not need benefits from a new employer? If so, this can lower your cost-of-hire to a new employer.

- Do you need specific benefits based on a loved one's needs?

- Vacation: How many weeks?

- Retirement programs: 401(k), pension, or another type?

- Are perks such as a company car, health club membership, country club membership, paid parking, and so on, a realistic expectation for your desired position?

- What is your overall threshold? Are you willing to be reasonable?

List your compensation and employee benefit considerations.

Reward System

 How do you want to be rewarded for positive performance? What kind of reward system would motivate you to perform? Compensation immediately comes to mind, but there are other considerations you may want to think about that could apply to you.

- Increase in salary
- Bonuses
- Stock options or equity
- Private recognition from management, peers, vendors, customers
- Public recognition—Awards banquets
- Increase of vacation and PTO in lieu of compensation increases
- Flexibility to work remotely—not having to be in the office
- Any other motivational factors that could be woven into a professional setting

Write down your reward system considerations.

Career Purpose

 What role will this next position play in your overall career? Contemplate what you want this position to accomplish. Here are some suggestions:

- What is the career goal for the position?
- What skills do you want to continue to utilize?
- What skills do you want to improve or learn?
- How important is stability (a company's size may influence your decision)?
- What role could this position play regarding your overall career plan?

Write down your career purpose considerations.

Other Considerations

These previous categories are by no means exhaustive. In fact, you have likely thought of a few considerations unique to your situation. Add to your list all of those considerations or aspirations that truly matter to you.

CREATE YOUR TARGET OPPORTUNITY PROFILE

 Pull it all together! You've done a lot of thinking and a lot of work. Good job! Start prioritizing your thoughts and considerations. What will emerge is your Target Opportunity Profile. When finished, you will have a guide—a profile—from which you can target and evaluate opportunities. You are now conducting a job search with a set of criteria, not based on emotion and gut feeling. Write down your Target Opportunity Profile.

JOB ALERTS

Job alerts can give you a flow of information about the job market. Websites like Indeed.com, SimplyHired.com, LinkedIn, Twitter, and industry specific job boards are good resources. Check into airsdirectory.com for industry and position specific job boards.

 Explore and then list websites or industry specific job boards where you will set up job alerts.

After exploring the websites and job boards, what job positions, qualifiers, and parameters will you use?

(Remember that job alerts are primarily used for information. If a position pops up that you are interested in, do not initially apply through the website. Identify the likely hiring executives and contact them directly first. Only apply through the website should direct contact fail.)

IN THE MIND OF THE EMPLOYER

There are a variety of reasons that can motivate an employer in a commercial setting to hire. The true essence underlying each reason is to either make or save the company money.

This is the first of several exercises that will begin to train your thinking on the value you can bring to an employer. What you write and list will translate and be used in later exercises in this workbook, just molded and expressed differently.

 Start thinking about all of your past jobs. How did your function make or save the company money? Here is a short list to get you thinking:

- Think about your duties and responsibilities from previous positions and how they translate to this position's ROI (Value, Return-On-Investment).

- Implementation of an improvement that saved time, efficiency, and streamlined workflow.

- Improved company image and branding.

- Opened new sales distribution channels.

- Improved a current product, or developed a new one.

- Expanded business/sales through existing accounts.

- Enhanced competitiveness through best practices, innovation, and so on.

- Improved client retention.

- Improved company culture, morale, and employee retention.

Write down how you have made or saved money for your employers. You will be able to refer back to this list whenever needed.

MASTER JOB DESCRIPTION

Shift gears now; go online and gather job postings for positions you are interested in (and qualified for). With these job postings (job descriptions) in hand, create your own Master Job Description by identifying common titles, themes, common requirements, and so on. What you will begin to see and learn is what employers are looking for and, with some insight, how they view the value and function of the position.

 Create your Master Job Description:

Through this exercise and writing assignment you should feel a shift in your view and understanding of the positions you've identified. As you begin to experience this change in perspective, you're thinking like an employer. This change in paradigm comes easier or more quickly to some than others. But, it will happen as you look at an open position through the eyes of the hiring executive tasked to fill it.

Now take the last critical step. Viewing the position through the eyes of the employer, what would you want to hear or see in a job seeker in filling the open position? Then, match and relate your professional experience in generating or saving money with the insight you have gained by creating your Master Job Description.

 Write down your experiences and accomplishments that correlate (match) what a hiring executive would want for the positions you're pursuing.

TRANSFERABLE SKILLS
AND PROFESSIONAL QUALITIES

Transferable Skills come in two forms. First are your technical skills (expertise and ability). The second are often referred to as "soft skills." Here is a list of some sought-after soft transferable skills: Communications skills (writing, listening, verbal), analytical ability, time management, innovation, collaboration, leadership, customer service, and business acumen.

Closely related to transferable soft skills is the concept of Professional Qualities. Here is a short list of professional qualities (character traits) sought by employers: honesty, positive attitude, interpersonal relationship skills, work ethic, dependability, and willingness to learn.

 What "soft" transferable skills do you have? What professional qualities do you possess? To help start your thinking, beyond those traits already listed, think about your last two or three positons. What skills did you use? Can you break any of those skills down into smaller components? Start your list of soft transferable skills. These are skills you can use regardless of job function or industry.

Think about your professional character traits, beyond those that were listed. What traits stand out that make you unique? What qualities would an employer value regardless of job function? List your professional qualities (professional character traits):

Once you have listed your transferable job skills and professional qualities, there are several areas in your job search where you will (can) use them. They can be:

- a component of your branding message
- woven into the summary section of your resume and LinkedIn profile
- mentioned in a Core Skills, experience, or accomplishments section of your resume
- used to write success stories
- used in cover letters and emails
- used as a part of your elevator speech
- used in networking conversations

List how you believe you will use your transferable job skills and professional qualities.

SUCCESS STORIES

Success Stories are a very persuasive job search tool. It is recommended that you write five to seven success stories that exemplify your top technical skills, soft transferable skills, and professional qualities.

There is a very easy formula to help you write success stories:

> C – Challenge (or situation)
>
> A – Action
>
> R – Result

 To help you with remembering things, think about projects, challenges, and problems you dealt with over your career, or even during a normal workweek or workday.

Here is the outline for your first success story:

Challenge:

Action (which reflects technical skills, transferable soft skills, and/or professional qualities):

Results:

BRANDING

Having a professional brand is very important. It announces who you are to the market and hiring executives.

The process of creating your brand requires thoughtful introspection. For some, it can be an emotional and professionally enlightening exercise.

 As you begin to think about what your professional brand is, start by asking yourself some questions:

1. What am I good at or an expert in?

2. What have I been recognized for?

3. What is my reputation with others (subordinates, peers, senior management)?

4. What have been my strong points in past job reviews (if applicable)?

5. What differentiates me from others with the same job?

6. What professional qualities do I have that make me good at my job?

7. What are the professional achievements I am most proud of?

8. What have been some consistent and notable comments made about me during job reviews?

Remember that transferable soft skills and professional qualities should also be listed.

Using the list and the thoughts they have provoked, create a one-sentence statement that captures (succinctly describes) who you are as a professional (e.g., Operational management professional dedicated to improving efficiency through effective leadership.)

ELEVATOR SPEECH

Having an effective and well-rehearsed elevator speech is a critical component to your job search. As you know, an elevator speech is a thirty-second speech that summarizes who you are, what you do, and the value you can bring to an employer.

 To create the foundation to your speech, follow these steps:

1. Identify yourself by function.

2. Write a one-sentence statement that describes your value proposition as a professional.

3. Construct an accomplishment or proof statement that supports your value proposition as a professional.

4. Write a summation of what you're looking for and a subtle invitation to have a conversation.

Your elevator speech should emphasize your brand—what you are good at. Here is an example:

Accounting: Focus on cost savings and technology

"I am a CPA who specializes in identifying cost-saving opportunities in manufacturing. With my former employer, I partially designed and implemented new technology and saved more than $750,000 over five years. The technology resulted in an increase in cash flow through accounts receivables and decreased collections. I want to make a job change to a manufacturing organization that can benefit from my abilities to use technology and identify cost-saving opportunities."

 Now, write your first draft of your elevator speech.

BUSINESS CARDS

Having business cards during a job search is a must. Circumstances will occur when you need to exchange contact information with a networking contact, colleague, hiring executive, and so on. *The Motivated Job Search* and *Over 50 and Motivated!* discuss four versions of business cards: traditional, networking, resume, and infographic ("networking handbill").

Which version(s) will you use?

Traditional _____

Networking _____

Resume _____

Infographic _____

 Use the space below to begin designing your business card(s) and the messaging you will use. Refer to *The Motivated Job Search* or *Over 50 and Motivated!* for additional guidance regarding the information on your business card.

RESUME

If you are starting from scratch or have not updated your resume in a long time, the thought of writing your resume can seem daunting. Regardless of what format you choose, the Resume Builder below will help you collect and organize your thoughts.

This section on building a resume and the following section on a LinkedIn profile work very closely together. There are common topics that overlap with common information. The best approach is to review the topics of both sections then start with resume topic knowing that the work you do here will likely apply, in large measure though not identically, for the LinkedIn section and vice versa.

 Given your work history and professional circumstances, which resume format are you likely to use?

Traditional Reverse Chronological _____

Functional _____

Showcase _____

Infographic _____

Resume Builder

Contact Information

Name:

Address: (Optional)

City:
State:
Zip:

Cell Phone:

Home Phone: (Optional)
Email:
URL (web portfolio, LinkedIn):

Title of Resume

List three or four titles you are qualified for. These position titles could be or be a part of the title of your resume.

1.

2.

3.

4.

Keywords

Keywords will be extremely important in your resume and job search. These are words that are relevant to your career experience and background. Keywords include your title, industry terms-of-art, professional designations, transferable skills, products and services, and so on. These words will be used with frequency on your resume, LinkedIn profile, and other written communications.

Having keywords on your resume is important because many employers use Applicant Tracking Software and input resumes into their systems. The software is able to search resumes by keywords.

 List what keywords best describe you professionally. Ask yourself: What words best describe my professional ability and qualifications? What is special about me and my background? What do I want to be known for or found for?

As you ponder your keywords, also think about what words an HR recruiter or hiring executive might use to find someone like you if they searched for you on LinkedIn or a company resume database.

The following are a few categories to start your thinking on keywords.

Title   Professional designations

Industry terms-of-art   Technical expertise/skills

Transferable skills   Professional qualities

Languages (IT or foreign)   Products/Services

Other keywords

Branding

Refer to the topic on Branding earlier in this workbook. Decide whether you want a branding statement or separate branding words to appear on your resume.

Explore the idea of using or manipulating what you've written (or will create) as your Headline for your LinkedIn profile. This can be a great starting point. Here's the formula:

[Job function or title] + [A bridge phrase (e.g. "with experience in," or "with expertise in," or "specializing in") or action verb] + [reference to products, services, skills, industry, professional qualities, etc.]

Example:
Senior Sales Executive with Experience in Workers' Compensation, Pain Management, Leadership

Example:
Product Development Professional Applying Behavioral Science to Healthcare Technology

 Write down your ideas that you can use for branding on your resume.

Career Summary

 Use this simple three-part formula to help you build the foundation for an impactful Career Summary:

1. A statement regarding your function or title.

2. A statement identifying your technical ability, qualifications, and accomplishments.

3. A statement regarding your transferable skills and/or professional traits.

    Example:
    A detailed-oriented CPA with over fifteen years of experience. Proven ability in financial forecasting and analysis, audit, reconciliation, tax law, and evaluating and consulting with clients regarding business investments and opportunities. Conscientious, self-motivated, and service-oriented professional who enjoys client interaction.

As a part of your career summary, you may choose to add a few career accomplishments too.

Accomplishments

Accomplishments will also be a significant component of your resume and job search. Accomplishments are specific measures of success involving your job. The most powerful accomplishments are frequently those with numbers and percentages. A commendation, written affirmation, or recommendation from your boss or client (or those you professionally interact with) can reflect as an accomplishment as well.

 List the most notable or influential accomplishments (including commendations, affirmations, and recommendations) you will use or reference on your resume and in your job search.

To start your thinking, consider these questions:

- Did you generate revenue for the company?
    - If so, by what amount? By what percentage?
    - Did you land any marquee clients? (Maybe you can list them.)
    - Did you upsell current clients with new products or services?

- Did you save your company money?
    - If so, how much? How did you achieve it?

- Did you save the company time through efficiency?
    - Can you measure and quantify it?

- Did you design and/or institute any new process?
    - If so, what were the results?

- Did you meet an impossible deadline through extra effort?
    - What difference did this make to your company?

- Did you bring a major project in under budget?
    - If so, by how much (use actual dollars or percentages)?

- Did you suggest and/or help launch a new product, program or initiative?
    - If so, did you take the lead or provide support?
    - How successful was the effort? Were there measurable outcomes?

- Did you take on new responsibilities that weren't part of your job?
    - If so, did you ask for the new projects or were they assigned to you?
    - What were the measurable results?

- Did you introduce any new or more effective techniques for increasing productivity?
  - What was the result?

- Did you improve "anything"?
  - If so, what was the outcome?
  - How did your company benefit?

Core Competencies

You may choose to have a section on your resume for Core Competencies. These are the key competencies that help you do your job. As you consider your core competencies, you may want to include your soft transferable skills and professional qualities.

 List your top eight to fifteen (no more than fifteen) core competencies.

Showcase Section

A showcase section is a section on your resume where you choose to highlight anything that you believe would be persuasive to a hiring executive. This could be accomplishments, special knowledge, certifications, marquee clients, distribution partners, and so on.

 One exercise to get you thinking would be to identify your top four professional skills with a corresponding achievement as proof of that skill.

Example:
Skill: Mentorship

Quantifiable achievements as proof of this skill: Over the last twelve years I have managed seven sales professionals who achieved our company's Pinnacle Award.

Skill #1:
Quantifiable achievements as proof of this skill:

Skill #2:
Quantifiable achievements as proof of this skill:

Skill #3:
Quantifiable achievements as proof of this skill:

Skill #4:
Quantifiable achievements as proof of this skill:

 What skills would you want to possibly highlight that would be persuasive to a hiring executive that you may want to include on your resume?

Recommendations

Occasionally, a short and impactful recommendation appearing on a resume can be persuasive.

 If you have a recommendation you'd like to include on your resume, locate it and write it down with the name of the person providing it (with title).

Employment History and Accomplishments

 As you consider each position, ask yourself: "How is this company better off now than when they hired me?" Quantify your results whenever possible. Review the accomplishments you listed previously.

Begin with **present employer**/project — include self-employment and volunteer or unpaid work if it applies.

Name of Company:

City/State:

Dates of Employment:

Your title or position:

Title of the person you reported to:

Number of people you supervised (as applicable):

Their titles or functions:

 Briefly describe the size of the organization (volume produced; revenues; number of employees; local, national, or international, etc.):

 Where do they rank in their industry in terms of their competitors?

Briefly describe your duties, responsibilities, level of authority. Use numbers (size) and percentages; quantify budgets, state with whom you interacted, etc.

 Why were you hired (or promoted or selected)? What was going on at the company? Was there a particular challenge or problem you were brought on to solve? Did you have specific performance measurements? If so, describe them as specifically as possible. Where was the company headed? Why did they need you?

 Describe accomplishments in this position.

Now repeat this process and answer the questions for each of your past employments.

 Now, with the information you have about each employment, determine how you will present each employment on your resume.

Education

Begin with your most recent and work backward.

    College/University:

    City/State:

    Major:

    Degree:

    Years:

    Scholarship (academic):

    Scholarship (athletic):

    Honors:

Repeat this for each post high school institution attended.

Other Information

Relevant industry-related courses/seminars/workshops: (include names, dates, place, sponsoring organization, etc.):

Certifications:

Professional Licenses (Do not include real estate license unless directly relevant to your career pursuit):

Professional Organizations/Affiliations (include offices held):

Publications / Presentations – Title / Periodical / Location / Date:

Computer Skills (includes operating systems, software, etc.):

Foreign Languages (fluency – verbal / written):

Community Activities (name of organization, years involved, positions held):

Additional Relevant Information:
(See sample resumes in *The Motivated Job Search* or *Over 50 and Motivated!*)

Resume Checklist

Once you have completed a working draft of your resume, evaluate it with the checklist below.

Item	Comments	Check-off √
Name	Given name, name you use (or both)	

Contact information
    Cell number
    Email address
	Double check for accuracy	

Title on resume	Functional or by position title	
Branding	A statement or separate branding words	
Summary	Use of skills, accomplishments, keywords	
Keywords	Titles, industry terms-of-art, professional designations and so on	
Showcase section(s)	Differentiation, awards, languages, marquee clients, patents, publications, etc.	
Experience	Listed in reverse chronological order	
Past employers	Note company name changes, one-sentence company descriptions	
Position titles	Include functional titles if titling is unique to employer	
Dates	Back fifteen years, then decide	
Duties/responsibilities	General guideline—four- to seven-sentence paragraphs describing duties and responsibilities	
Accomplishments	Use numbers, percentages whenever possible, statement of affirmation can work also	
Education	Highest degree first; list in reverse chronological order	
Other sections	Volunteering, licenses, associations, other noteworthy information	
What NOT to include	Age, marital status, health, social security number, income, religion, politics, references upon-request	

Appearance
    Font use
    Margins
    Bold, italics lettering
	Pleasing, consistent, easy-on-the-eyes	

Volume of information	Enough to inform and differentiate, not too much Not your professional autobiography	
Length	Two pages (recommended)	

LINKEDIN PROFILE

Information contained on your LinkedIn profile will closely align with your resume. However, there are differences in content and the strategic use and placement of information.

As we move through this topic, not every section of a LinkedIn profile will be specifically discussed. Many of the fields or boxes on the LinkedIn profile are self-explanatory. Only the topics that have special considerations will be discussed. Refer to *The Motivated Job Search* or *Over 50 and Motivated!* for specific instructions.

Photo

 Do you have a professionally taken photo for your profile? Or a close-up of you professionally dressed? ___Yes ___No (Profiles with photos get fourteen times more views)

Name

 Consider the following:

Will you use only your birth name?
Will you use the name you commonly go by?
Will you display a significant professional designation after your last name?
Write down your name as it will appear on your LinkedIn profile.

Headline

This is the area under your name where you can use branding and keywords to increase your discoverability by HR recruiters and others. Refer to the branding topic in this workbook and *The Motivated Job Search* or *Over 50 and Motivated!* job search books. A very useful formula that works for many job seekers is:

[Job function or title] + [A bridge phrase (e.g., "with experience in," or "with expertise in," or "specializing in") or action verb] + [reference to products, services, skills, industry, professional qualities, etc.]

You have 120 characters (which is actually quite a few) to communicate your brand and what you want to be known for or found for.

 Write down your Headline.

Keywords

Keywords are extremely important in your LinkedIn profile. As previously mentioned, these are words that are relevant to your career experience and background.

 Refer to the keywords you listed previously in the workbook and make sure they appear frequently in your LinkedIn profile.

Summary

To make your LinkedIn profile more find-able, you will use your keywords in your summary. The number of times your chosen keywords appear affects your find-ability. Use this technique: Make the first sentence of your summary virtually identical to your headline, but expand it. It will appear like a banner and introduce the reader to the rest of the summary.

 Write down what the first line of your summary (your banner statement) will be.

As you formulate the rest of your Summary, consider following this three-part formula as the foundational pillars in creating your summary:

1. A statement regarding your function or title.

2. A statement identifying your technical ability, qualifications, and accomplishments.

3. A statement regarding your transferable skills and/or professional traits.

It can be good strategy to include your top three or four career accomplishments in your summary. This can help make your profile compelling to the reader. ("Compelling" in that it motivates the reader to contact you.) Write down your top career accomplishments that you could include in your summary.

 Using your professional judgment, you may choose to include a list of core competencies in your summary. If you elect to do so, list your top competencies.

Experience

 For each position, describe your duties and responsibilities in four to six sentences (general guideline). Then list your accomplishments using numbers and percentages when possible. Write down how each employment position will appear on your LinkedIn profile.

Education

List your education in reverse chronological order with your highest degree listed first. For tenured job seekers, consider omitting dates. Unless there is a valid strategic reason, high school should not be listed.

 Write down how your education section will appear on your profile.

Recommendations

Recommendations can enhance the completeness and overall positive impact of your profile. Having a minimum of three good recommendations is best practice.

 List who you could request a recommendation from, if you need additional recommendations.

Skills (and Endorsements)

As you think about the skills you have listed (or will list), think about your technical abilities, transferable skills, and professional qualities. Listing professional qualities (professional character traits) is unique on a LinkedIn profile. Listing one or two, then receiving endorsements for them, will differentiate you from other job seekers.

 List the skills (technical, transferable, and professional qualities) that will appear on your profile.

Interests

The Interests section of your profile is important for reasons that you may be unaware of. For example, when an HR recruiter performs a search on LinkedIn, the LinkedIn programming and algorithms search the Interests box for matching keywords. Consequently, it is important to include your business interests using your chosen keywords in the Interests box. This will notably increase your find-ability (ranking of matching profiles). You can also include your personal interests as well, but business interests, using your keywords, must be included and should be listed first.

 Write down what will appear in your Interests box.

Completeness

The more complete your LinkedIn profile is, the higher it will rank compared to other profiles. LinkedIn has additional sections that can be added to your profile beyond those that are most commonly used. They include: Language, Volunteering Opportunities, Honors and Awards, Test Scores, Courses, Patents, Causes You Care About, Supported Organizations, Projects, Personal Details, Certifications (Professional Designations), Publications, Contact Information, Organizations (Professional Associations and Affiliations), Posts.

 Identify what other sections apply to you and what information you will use.

LinkedIn: High Impact Checklist

Making your LinkedIn profile complete and impactful is very important to your job search. Below is a checklist that will increase the impact of your profile and your find-ability when HR recruiters and hiring executives go looking for you.

Item	Comments	Check-off √
A profile	Do you actually have one . . . an easy check-off	
Name	Use the name you go by, add professional designation	
Photo	Professionally taken or close up	
Headline	A statement or separate branding words, use keywords, mention skills	
Location	Your metropolitan area	
Industry	Choose the best one for you	
Contact information	Filled out	
Keywords	Words you want to be known for or found for. Place in headline, summary, experience, skills, and interests box	
Summary Section	Banner Statement, then as a general guideline four- to seven-sentence paragraphs. Use keywords, accomplishments, core competencies. Enough to inform and differentiate. Not your professional autobiography.	
Experience	Back fifteen years, then decide	
Job titles	Functional or actual position title, titles are keywords	
Employment	Listed in reverse chronological order. Note company name changes, one-sentence company descriptions, duties and responsibilities, and accomplishments.	
Accomplishments	Specific measurements of success. Goes to the compelling nature of your profile.	
Education	Highest degree first; list in reverse chronological order	
Certifications	Goes to differentiation and qualifications	
Professional organizations	Shows professional and industry involvement, network	
Endorsements	Others endorsing you for your skills, no more than 15 skills	
Involvement	Volunteer, causes	
Recommendations	As many as reasonably possible, minimum of three	
Interests section	Include business interests (that's important), use keywords	
Other areas	Use as applicable—publications, languages, patents, etc.	
Connections	Get to 50, then work to get to 500	
LinkedIn URL—customize	Changed to reflect your name without programming jargon	

Item	Comments	Check-off √
Multi-media	Adds depth to your profile	
Groups	Join those that are applicable to you	
Information not on your profile	Age, marital status, health, social security number, income, religion, politics	
Job Alerts	Set up job alerts on LinkedIn	
Open Candidates Feature	Activate Open Candidates feature on LinkedIn	

TWITTER: CREATING YOUR BIO

For those who are new to Twitter, you will need to write a Twitter bio. This bio is important because it is what others will first read about you on Twitter.

You are allotted 160 characters to present yourself and your brand. So brevity is king! To get you thinking, go back and review your LinkedIn profile, elevator speech, branding message, and network/resume business cards. Pick out key words and phrases that you want announced in your bio. Then start formulating your bio. Explore other Twitter profiles for ideas if needed.

Here are a couple of partial example profiles to get you thinking:

> *Award-winning care management sales professional . . .*

> *Accomplished operational management executive . . .*

 Remember that you only have 160 characters. Keep it impactful and tight! Write your Twitter bio.

Twitter for Job Alerts

Twitter has a functionality that allows you to set up tightly defined job alerts through Twitter. Here's how: Go into your Twitter account. Go to the search field at the top of the page and type in: search.twitter.com. Hit enter.

Then go to the More Options tab. You will get a drop-down menu. At the bottom is an option for Advanced Search. Go there and enter. You are now in the advanced search function.

Enter the words: Jobs, Hiring, Employment, and other job search keywords, job titles, or phrases. Enable your location (or not). Then save the search.

 Write the titles and keywords you will use if you choose to use Twitter for job alerts.

FACEBOOK

Facebook is generally viewed more as a "social," friends, and family networking platform. This is not to imply that its use as a job search tool is diminished. It's not. It only means your connections will likely be different than your professional connections on LinkedIn.

The use of Facebook in your job search will be more a referral source. Your contacts (with exceptions, of course) will help you spread the word and help you find job leads more than potentially hire you.

If you choose to use Facebook as a tool in your job search, you may need to rewrite your bio. Since your connections are likely acquaintances, friends, and family, it's a good idea to write your bio with some personality. Don't be too business-like.

 A good starting point for your bio would be your LinkedIn headline. Manipulate that statement to craft an appropriate Facebook bio.

NETWORKING

Networking will be vitally important to your job search. It is estimated that 60 to 80 percent of all jobs are found by networking.[1] Furthermore, surveys indicate that job seekers who are referred to a hiring executive have a 1 in 7 chance of landing a job offer compared to 1 in 100 if they apply online.[2] Getting referred to a job is a function of networking.

 Since networking is so vitally important to your job search, take some time and seriously evaluate the "health" and potential usefulness of your current network. Do you (really) have enough quality, relevant contacts to drive your job search? Evaluate your network by asking yourself the questions below. Give yourself one point for each "yes." (Be an honest, hard grader):

1. Is your professional network comprised predominantly of people within your industry or position type? __Yes   __No

2. Does it contain connections that can lead you to other connections that have influence, perhaps even potential hiring executives? __Yes   __No

3. Do you feel your professional network is large enough? __Yes   __No

1 LinkedIn, "Using LinkedIn to Find a Job"; Beatty, "The Math Behind the Networking Claim"; Rothberg, "80% of Job Openings."

2 Jobvite Social Recruiting Survey 2012, http://web.jobvite.com/rs/jobvite/images/Jobvite_2012_Social_Recruiting_Survey.pdf.

4. Are you a member of enough industry-specific LinkedIn groups, associations, or relevant local groups? __Yes   __No

5. Do you feel your network can help you? __Yes   __No

How did you do?

5 points. Great job on your network!

4 points. Your network is excellent but could stand some improvement.

3 points. You need to spend time building your network.

2 points. Your network needs serious attention.

0 or 1 point. Get your network a lifeline, stat!

Now, for every question you answered "no" and for every question you felt any uncertainty answering "yes," focus your networking efforts on those areas.

Here's a concept you need to ponder. No one really has a perfect "5" network. Over time, contacts in your network will come and go. Their level of influence will change. New people enter the scene without you even knowing it. Always be actively cultivating and expanding your network regardless of whether you are in a job search.

 Now that you have critically evaluated your network, write down the action steps that you will take to improve it.

Your Networking Cabinet

As a part of your networking efforts, you should know who is in your Cabinet. A Cabinet is a small group of truly trusted advisors in whom you have unwavering belief that they will help you in any reasonable way possible. These are your "go-to" people. These people should easily come to mind, but occasionally one could slip through the cracks.

 Write down the names of those trusted contacts that you believe belong in your Cabinet. (Remember, these are people you are virtually 100% sure will help you and have your best interests at heart.)

Networking—Local Market Contacts

For local, non-industry-specific job searches, networking with those who rely on networking for their livelihood and those who are well connected as a result of their community involvement are great resources. These include real estate agents, financial planners, accountants, civic leaders, as well as those involved in philanthropic endeavors.

 List people you know who are in these lines of work that you can reach out to regarding your job search.

Networking at Conferences and Events:
Icebreaker Questions

Frequently, the most uncomfortable and intimidating part about face-to-face networking at an event is starting a conversation. It's an awkward situation. The trick to overcoming the discomfort and potential anxiety is to prepare a handful of conversation starters—otherwise known as icebreakers.

Here are a few generic icebreaker questions:

What do you do? Follow this question with a request for their opinion, their take on an industry issue, trend, event, etc.

What motivated you to come to this conference/event?

What do you think of the lineup of speakers?

What did you think of the last speaker?

What are you finding most interesting [or valuable] about the conference?

Attendance looks good. Do you come every year?

What's keeping you [or their company] busy these days?

Do not brush off this exercise with the belief that you can think of a question on the fly. Do the preparation work of thinking of insightful icebreaker questions in advance. As you know, first impressions mean a lot! Having a well-thought-out icebreaker question designed for the networking event can score big points with your networking contact. If it is a local networking event, think of something that is going on locally to bring up as a conversation starter. If it is a trade conference, ask for opinions about issues and trends that could start a conversation.

 Now write a few insightful or engaging icebreaker questions for any upcoming or foreseeable networking event.

RECRUITERS

Recruiters can be a valuable resource during a job search. The key is finding the ones who can help you and advance your search. *The Motivated Job Search* and *Over 50 and Motivated!* cover several techniques you can use to identify recruiters. These include calling hiring executives, calling colleagues, and finding recruiters on LinkedIn, the Internet, and directories.

 List the names of 5 to 10 recruiters you have discovered from your research. Contact them. Consider inviting them to connect on LinkedIn.

1.

2.

3.

4.

5.

6.

7.

8.

9.

10.

PROACTIVELY MARKETING YOUR PROFESSIONAL CREDENTIALS

Proactively marketing your professional credentials to potential employers dives straight into the heart of the Hidden Job Market. It can be very effective, but it requires work. The concept behind this approach, in large part, is to stop looking for a job but start looking for a good company to work for.

 One of the first steps in this process is identifying potential employers. Sources could include:

1. Competitors of your current or past employer(s)

2. Companies where your LinkedIn contacts work

3. Companies you can identify by reviewing profiles on a LinkedIn group

4. Association membership lists

5. Industry conference attendee lists and vendor lists

6. Clients, suppliers, and distributors of your current/past employer

7. Books of Lists with major employers by industry type (most metropolitan areas have them)

8. Purchased lists (services that sell databases of companies and contacts) including:
   - www.infousa.com
   - www.hoovers.com
   - www.standardandpoors.com

– www.jigsaw.com
– www.listgiant.com
– www.goleads.com
– www.vault.com

 Although you have a lot of work to be done in creating this list, start with a short list of employers that immediately come to mind, then build from there.

Scripting Your Marketing Call

Proactively marketing your professional credentials will require you to make phone calls. Knowing in advance what you are going to say takes much of the anxiety out of generating the call. The script you are going to write is centered around the scenario of you calling a hiring executive and getting the opportunity to speak with him or her.

Introduction

The introduction identifies who you are. If you can, reference a mutual business colleague or business association. That common ground often helps break the ice.

> *"Mr. Tyrrell, my name is Gene Watson. I was referred to you by Bob Johnson."*
>
> *"Mr. Tyrrell, my name is Gene Watson, and I am a care management sales professional. I don't believe we've spoken before, however, we both belong to the (care management association)."*

If you do not have a common reference point:

> *"Mr. Tyrrell, my name is Gene Watson. I am a care management sales professional, and I am currently (or formerly) with (Company Name)."*

Ask permission to continue the call

Hiring executives are busy, and they will appreciate the thoughtfulness.

> *"I realize that I've called you out of the blue. Did I catch you at a good time?"*
>
> *"I hope that I can get a few minutes of your time?"*

Get their attention

As with your elevator speech, make a clear statement about one of your showcase accomplishments. Grab the hiring executive's attention.

> *"I am a care management sales professional, and for the last four years I exceeded sales quotas by 27 percent. My sales have been achieved by selling through fee-for-service consultants, payers, and directly to larger companies."*

> *"I am an underwriting management professional, and with my previous employer I rewrote the underwriting guidelines, which resulted in the growth of our block of business from $25M to $80M over four years."*

Purpose for the call

Now that you have introduced yourself and gotten the hiring executive's attention, state the reason for the call . . . to set up an interview.

> *"I'm looking to make a career move, and I would like to meet (or speak) with you to discuss how I can contribute to the success of (Company Name)."*

Relate to the employer (optional)

If possible, try to make a statement (if you can) that relates to the employer. This can be a statement specific to the company, a trend, or an issue facing the industry.

> *"By the way, I understand that you have just rolled out a new cost containment service line."*
> *"As we both know, the new regulations that take effect next year are going to complicate business."*

If you do not have enough information about the company or industry, you can omit the "relate" portion of the script.

Close

Close the script with a request for an interview (the ultimate purpose of the call).

> *"I am available [to meet with you or speak with you in more detail] in the afternoons next week. Which day would work best for you?"* OR *"I can make myself available Tuesday morning or after 3 p.m. on Thursday. Which timeframe might work best for you?"*
> Or a less-assumptive approach, *"I am available generally in the afternoons next week if you would be interested in [meeting] speaking further."*

 Using the above example as a guide, write your Marketing Call Script.

Preparing for Objections

It is inevitable that as you speak with hiring executives, you will hear objections or deflections to what you've said (your script). Anticipate it and prepare for it. There are four common objections. Having prepared responses will keep your engagement smooth and conversational. You wouldn't be knocked off your game.

 The Motivated Job Search and *Over 50 and Motivated!* **contain sample responses. Use them as guides in crafting your responses to each of these four objections.**

1. "I don't have any openings."

2. "Can you send me your resume?"

3. "I really don't have time to talk right now."

4. "You'll need to speak with Talent Acquisition (Human Resources)."

One technique that occasionally can spur a conversation is to ask one question after the objection. Write down one or two questions you could feel comfortable asking after you respond to the objection.

What to Say to a Gatekeeper

As you make your calls, you will encounter gatekeepers—a person whose function is to protect the hiring executive's time. Be friendly to these people. One way to gain access through the gatekeeper is to have a prepared statement for when they ask: "What is this regarding?" One example response:

> *"I am an industrial engineer. I am exploring a career move, and I am connected to Earl (the hiring executive) on LinkedIn. I am following up on an Inmail I sent. Is he available?"*

 Write down two or three responses you can use in response to a gatekeeper's screening question.

Voicemail Message

As you call hiring executives and market your professional credentials, you will leave a lot of voicemail messages. Your voicemail message must be pre-written, rehearsed, and delivered in a well-paced and articulate way.

Here is an example of an effective voicemail message in addition to the example in *The Motivated Job Search* and *Over 50 and Motivated!*:

> *"Kathy, this is Toni Sanders, and I am a post-sales account management professional who has maintained a 95% retention rate on my client block of business. I would like to speak with you at your convenience to explore how I can contribute to your client relationship department of LPC, LLC. I can be reached at: 123-456-7890."*

 Write your voicemail message (then say it out loud a few times to rehearse. You might choose to change things to make it sound smoother.)

Cover Letters

To maximize your success when writing cover letters, use the Cover Letter Success Formula laid out in *The Motivated Job Search* and *Over 50 and Motivated!* The formula is:

Create interest

Match

Showcase accomplishments/qualifications

Additional information

Close

The Motivated Job Search and *Over 50 and Motivated!* go into detail regarding the Cover Letter Success Formula.

 Start crafting a template cover letter that you can customize during your job search.

Marketing Your Professional Credentials
by Email (or InMail)

Depending upon your circumstances and professional judgement, you may choose to initially communicate with the hiring executives by email (or LinkedIn Inmail). Marketing emails essentially follow the identical Cover Letter Success Formula referenced above and in *The Motivated Job Search* and *Over 50 and Motivated!* There is one particularly important item that requires some serious thought—the Subject Line.

To be truly effective, your subject line must be eye-catching (impactful in some way) and short. If you were hiring for your desired position, what subject line would catch your attention?

A very good approach is using your Headline from your LinkedIn profile, and then modifying it, as needed, using your professional judgment.

 Write a couple of possible subject lines that you might use when marketing your professional credentials by email (or InMail).

Below is a sample marketing email. This email presumes that you have no knowledge of whether there is an open position suitable for your skills. Pattern yours in a similar way, or fashion a new way keeping in mind the Cover Letter Success Formula:

1. Create interest
2. Match
3. Showcase an accomplishment / qualification
4. Additional information
5. Close

Example:

Subject line: Top Flight Healthcare Solutions Sales Professional

Karyn (hiring executive's first name, or Ms. Johnson),

I am an experienced Healthcare Solutions Sales Professional who has led my company in sales four of the last five years. In fact, my sales production accounts for more than 50% of the new business sales for each of those years! I am exploring a career move.

I have a respected reputation in the industry and established relationships in the large employer market and with national fee-for-service consultants. I am looking to convert those relationships to my next employer. My business contacts are predominantly in the middle third of the country.

My product knowledge covers a wide array of products and services, including wellness, population health, behavioral health, decision support, transparency, consumer-driven healthcare, benefits administration, and traditional group insurance.

One of my references states:

From my many years of working with [your name] as a manager and colleague, she is one of a very select group of people who is the "Complete Package." She has industry knowledge, character, integrity, thoroughness, work ethic, and she gets results!

Senior Vice President Sales
Healthcare Services Company

I am looking for a sales opportunity in the healthcare solutions/technology sector with a stable and growing organization that has a vision or a value proposition that differentiates it from the market.

If you should have an interest or a need for a proven and accomplished sales professional who can capitalize on current relationships, please reply or call me.

Best Regards,

 Now, begin constructing your template marketing email. You'll customize your emails to certain employers based on special information you may have or research you have done.

Your "interest" statement:

"Matching" statement:

Showcase accomplishments/qualifications:

Additional information:

Close:

It is important to remember to call the hiring executive after a few days if you do not hear back.

Drip Email Marketing

An effective strategy that can be blended into your proactive marketing efforts is "drip marketing." The drip concept is sending a marketing-styled email containing new information systematically over a period of time. Although you have a lot of discretion on what to send and how often to send it, the technique can be used when you are not getting a response or when you have a response but a decision on the next steps or when the position will be filled is unclear. In that event, your well-timed drip marketing can keep your name top-of-mind.

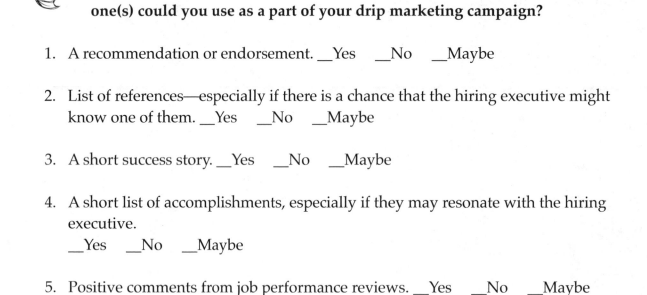 *The Motivated Job Search* **and** *Over 50 and Motivated!* **list several ideas. Which one(s) could you use as a part of your drip marketing campaign?**

1. A recommendation or endorsement. __Yes   __No   __Maybe

2. List of references—especially if there is a chance that the hiring executive might know one of them. __Yes   __No   __Maybe

3. A short success story. __Yes   __No   __Maybe

4. A short list of accomplishments, especially if they may resonate with the hiring executive.
    __Yes   __No   __Maybe

5. Positive comments from job performance reviews. __Yes   __No   __Maybe

6. An abridged summary from a personality assessment. __Yes   __No   __Maybe

7. A list of marquee clients or distribution channel partners (or contacts) if you're in sales or account management. __Yes   __No   __Maybe

When All Else Fails—Your Last-Ditch Effort

Despite your best efforts and use of all reasonable techniques, there will be some hiring executives who simply will not respond ... even if it were just to say "No thanks."

When this happens, consider sending one last closing email. Here is an example:

> *Anita,*
>
> *I've reached out to you a few times over the past week or so. I'm sorry we have not connected. By the way, congratulations on your recent acquisition!*
>
> *I am an operations professional in the plastics industry. I managed four manufacturing facilities in four separate regions and exceeded production and profit goals for the last five consecutive years.*
>
> *I am in a job search looking for a senior operations position in the plastics or rubber industries based in the South (Texas would be ideal).*
>
> *Should you become aware of any positions that could be a match, feel free to pass along my information. My resume is attached.*
>
> *Best Wishes,*
> *Your Name*

 Using this as a guide to your thinking, write your "When All Else Fails" email.

Unique Tactics That Create Differentiation

The Motivated Job Search and *Over 50 and Motivated!* list several unique tactics that create differentiation. They include: a Brag Book, Career Summary Sheet, Testimonial Sheet, and an Action Plan. In addition to these, there is also the creation of a Personal Website, a Blog, and an Infographic Resume (and infographic business card/handbill).

 As you think through your job search, which of these unique tactics might you use in your job search? (Be mindful of the time commitment for each tactic.)

Brag Book _____

Career Summary Sheet _____

Testimonial Sheet _____

Action Plan _____

Personal Website _____

A Blog _____

An Infographic Resume _____

An Infographic Business Card/Handbill _____

INTERVIEWING

The Motivated Job Search and *Over 50 and Motivated!* list a lot of things you need to do to prepare for interviews. One of the more important is scripting answers to questions you know or reasonably believe could be asked of you. There are a handful of questions that seem to be asked in most interviews. Refer to *The Motivated Job Search* or *Over 50 and Motivated!* for guidance in crafting your answers.

 Script responses to these questions below:

Tell me about yourself and your background.

Why are you looking for a job change?

What are your strengths?

What are your weaknesses?

Why are you interested in our company? What do you know about our company? (You can't pre-script an answer, but be aware that this is likely going to be asked.)

This next exercise requires you to "sit on the other side of the desk." Critically look at your resume and formulate questions you would ask yourself if you were the hiring executive. What questions would you likely ask as the hiring executive? This could include behavior-based questions, questions about job moves, and so on. As you think of these questions, write them down and script an answer you would give. You could come up with several questions. Think in the mind of the hiring executive.

 Write down likely questions and script a response.

Question 1:

Question 2:

Question 3:

Question 4:

Question 5:

Question 6:

Question 7:

Explanations (Scripting) for: Job Termination, Employment Gaps, Long-term Unemployment, and Job Hops

If you have been terminated, have employment gaps, experienced long-term unemployment, or job hops, you will be asked about it in interviews. *The Motivated Job Search* and *Over 50 and Motivated!* provide guidance on how to handle these situations.

 Script what you will say when asked about these situations. Your script should answer any questions without unnecessary details.

Post-Interview Debrief Form

 After every interview, debrief yourself and evaluate your performance. Debriefing yourself will help you evaluate your performance and improve. *The Motivated Job Search* and *Over 50 and Motivated!* provide an explanation for each question, but here are the questions to ask yourself.

1. *How long did the interview last?*

2. *What things did I do well?*

3. *Was I unprepared for any questions? If so, what were they?*

4. *What were some of the key issues that were brought up during the interview?*

5. *What did I learn during my research and interview that appeals to me about the position?*

6. *Identify any concerns and negatives.*

7. *Rate (emotionally) the opportunity on a scale of one to ten. How do you feel about it?*

8. *Was compensation discussed? If so, what was said?*

9. *How was it left?*

10. *How do I rank this opportunity against others I am pursuing?*

11. *Was there anything I could have done better or differently?*

REFERENCES

References can significantly influence the hiring decision. They can appeal to the persuasion principles of authority, liking, and social proof.

As you think about your references, think about people who can attest to different aspects of your professional experience, professional skills (hard and soft), as well as your professional qualities. Thinking through this in advance can save time. For example, let's say that some themes of an interview were technical skills and the professional quality of integrity. Who do you know that could speak, with examples based on experience, to your technical skills? Who could attest to your integrity and honesty? It could be two different people.

 Take some time and think about your skills and qualities. Who can be a reference for each?

Identify your references below.

Skill or Professional Quality:

Name of Reference:

Skill or Professional Quality:

Name of Reference:

Skill or Professional Quality:

Name of Reference:

Skill or Professional Quality:

Name of Reference:

Skill or Professional Quality:

Name of Reference:

EVALUATING A JOB OFFER

There can be a lot of soul searching when it comes to evaluating a job offer. How does the opportunity compare to your Target Opportunity Profile? How do you feel about the people you will be working for/with? How do you feel about the totality of the opportunity?

One of the things that occasionally gets overlooked is getting complete job offer information or details. Below is a non-exhaustive checklist to get you thinking and help you gather information.

___ Salary

___ Insurance—health, life, disability, dental

___ 401(k)—retirement plan

___ Bonus pay, structure, factors regarding how to earn bonuses

___ Salary adjustments—timing of performance reviews and percentage

___ Relocation expenses (if applicable)

___ Tuition assistance (including continuing education)

___ Vacation or Personal Time Off (PTO)

___ Commissions structure, incentive compensation

___ Equipment: car, cell phone, computer, office equipment for home office, and so on

___ Parking expenses

___ Professional organization membership dues

___ Stock options/stock grants

___ Memberships (country club or fitness)

___ Severance package

___ Anything else you can think of

Once you believe you have complete information, and should you believe it necessary, write down your assessment and feelings about the offer and the opportunity. You can make it a pros and cons list if you like. Writing down your assessment, pros, cons, and feelings will help you clarify your thinking so you don't keep rethinking the same thing over and over, believing you are critically evaluating the offer.

 Write down your evaluation, pros, cons, and feelings.